The Power of Yes

David Hare was born in Sussex in 1947. Sixteen of his plays have been produced at the National Theatre, including a trilogy about the Church, the Law and the Labour Party – *Racing Demon*, *Murmuring Judges* and *The Absence of War* – which played in repertory in the Olivier Theatre in 1993. Ten of his best-known plays, including *Plenty*, *The Secret Rapture*, *Skylight*, *The Blue Room*, *Amy's View*, *The Judas Kiss*, *Via Dolorosa* – in which he performed – and *The Vertical Hour* have also been presented on Broadway. His most recent screenplays are for the films of *The Hours* and *The Reader*.

DAVID HARE

The Power of Yes

*A dramatist seeks to understand
the financial crisis*

faber and faber

First published in 2009
by Faber and Faber Limited
74–77 Great Russell Street
London WC1B 3DA

Typeset by Country Setting, Kingsdown, Kent CT14 8ES
Printed in England by CPI Bookmarque, Croydon, Surrey

A CIP record for this book
is available from the British Library

ISBN 978-0-571-25468-2

2 4 6 8 10 9 7 5 3 1

The Power of Yes was first presented in the Lyttelton auditorium of the National Theatre, London, on 29 September 2009, with the following cast:

The Author Anthony Calf
Masa Serdarevic Jemima Rooper
Myron Scholes Malcolm Sinclair
George Soros Bruce Myers
A Leading Industrialist Richard Cordery
Harry Lovelock Simon Williams
Deborah Solomon Lizzie Winkler
David Marsh Jeff Rawle
Young Man at the Bank Christian Roe
Howard Davies Jonathan Coy
Paul Hammond Ian Bartholomew
Jon Cruddas MP Nicolas Tennant
Scott Rudmann Peter Sullivan
David Freud Ian Gelder
Ronald Cohen Paul Freeman
Adair Turner Malcolm Sinclair
Jon Moulton Ian Gelder
A Northern Echo Journalist John Hollingworth
Paul Mason Nicolas Tennant
The Chair of a Mortgage Lender Richard Cordery
A Hedge Fund Manager Ian Bartholomew
A Financial Times Journalist Claire Price
Simon Loftus John Hollingworth
Tom Huish Jeff Rawle
Ensemble Julien Ball, Mark Elstob, Alan Vicary

Director Angus Jackson
Designer Bob Crowley
Lighting Designer Paule Constable
Music Stephen Warbeck
Projection Designer Jon Driscoll with Gemma Carrington
Sound Designer John Leonard
Researcher Masa Serdarevic

Characters

The Author
Masa Serdarevic
Myron Scholes, *an academic*
George Soros, *a philanthropist*
A Leading Industrialist
Harry Lovelock, *a lawyer*
Deborah Solomon, *a journalist*
David Marsh, *a banker*
Alan Greenspan
former Chairman of the Federal Reserve Board
Young Man at the Bank
Howard Davies
first Chair of the Financial Services Authority
Paul Hammond, *a financial head-hunter*
Jon Cruddas MP
Scott Rudmann, *a private equity investor*
David Freud, *a government adviser and banker*
Ronald Cohen, *a private equity pioneer*
Adair Turner
Chair of the Financial Services Authority
Jon Moulton, *a private equity investor*
A Northern Echo Journalist
Paul Mason, *a television journalist*
The Chair of a Mortgage Lender
A Hedge Fund Manager
A Financial Times Journalist
Simon Loftus, *a bond trader*
Tom Huish, *Adviser, Citizens Advice Bureau*

THE POWER OF YES

For Juliette and Madeleine

'The laws of commerce are the laws of nature,
and therefore the laws of God.'

Edmund Burke

'If you want good security, hire a thief.'

*Financial recruiter,
explaining why disgraced bankers
are being offered new jobs*

ONE

*One moment, the stage is empty. Next moment, the whole
company appears, shimmering. There is one younger
woman, and one older, but otherwise they are all men in
suits – ranks of them. The Author, a tall man, sixties,
speaks.*

Author This isn't a play. It's a story. Or rather it's only
partly a play. It's more properly a story. And what a
story! How capitalism came to a grinding halt. Where
were you on September 15th 2008? Do you remember?
Did you notice? Capitalism ceased to function for about
four days.

This summer I set out to find out what had happened.

TWO

*Music. Many things happen at once. A bristle-haired man
(Jon M) in his fifties leans back in his chair to a more or
less horizontal position. A man (David M) with his tie
over his shoulder puts his elbows on the table.
A gleaming man in his seventies (George), with a slight
Hungarian accent, reaches for sparkling water. A man in
his sixties (the Chair of a Mortgage Lender) with a
problem in his legs gets up and starts shaking them. A man
in his sixties (Harry) sits back. A woman in her thirties
(a Financial Journalist) gets up to pour coffee. A man in
his late thirties, American, in jeans and blazer (Scott) takes
several phones from his pockets. A short man in his sixties
(David F) puts his hands behind his head. A tall man
(Ronald), sixties, elegant, starts walking round. A man*

in a Jermyn Street shirt, in his fifties (Paul), practises a few golf shots. A bald man in his fifties (Howard) taps at his computer screen. The Author has a black notebook, writes sometimes, mostly listens.

Jon M I've been thinking about how to do a play about this and you're welcome to my creative thought if you want it.

David M By the time your play comes out the whole thing's going to be over.

George I would have thought your problem as a playwright is that it's a big event, but it's an abstract event.

David M The banking crisis will be interesting as anthropology but not much else. How on earth do you bring to life securitised debt arrangements?

George However, I leave that side of things to you.

Author Thank you. At last someone who trusts me.

Chair of Mortgage Lender Please don't end up writing a play in which you say bankers are a load of shits. Because then you'll be writing what people already think, and it'll be a very dull play.

David M I can see why you're going to have problems.

Chair of Mortgage Lender Why tell people what they already believe? What's the point of that?

Author No point.

Harry I saw your previous plays, *Stuff Happens* and *The Permanent Way*, and OK, you may say, in Iraq and on the railways, people died. And this time nobody has died. But there's a long, long way to go.

David M I wrote a book about the euro, and personally I think it's an extremely gripping story, but I have had

4

trouble persuading everyone that it's as exciting as I think it is.

Harry We haven't begun to absorb the most significant financial catastrophe in British history.

George Alan Greenspan, now he's an interesting character. You could write a whole play about him.

David M Greenspan's a wonderful villain, now there's your villain for you . . .

George You know he's obsessed with Ayn Rand?

Author I didn't know that.

George Ayn Rand? The novelist? He's obsessed!

Financial Journalist If you need a villain, you're not going to do better than Fred Goodwin.

Scott Fucking Fred Goodwin! What a jerk! Cowboy! What fucking cheek! For shame! *For shame!*

Paul Gordon Brown's the villain, I would have thought that was obvious. This all happened under a Labour government. It didn't happen under a Conservative government.

Harry We won't be out of this till 2025. Can you imagine?

Jon M To me Brown's like the captain of a ship and when he runs into the rocks, he gets into the lifeboat. Then when the lifeboat springs a leak, he says, 'I know what to do,' and he sticks his bum in the hole. Really. I believe he has behaved in a way which is unethical – profoundly unethical.

Chair of Mortgage Lender If it's a play, it's a Greek tragedy. You're going along in a dream, then the Furies arrive and boy, do they wake you up!

Ronald The whole thing is a complete and utter fuck-up.

Howard I think of the whole thing as a Shakespearian tragedy, and like all great tragedies it ends with bodies all over the stage.

Ronald Without heroes.

Paul If you do write a play, make it a comedy. If it's serious it'll just be political crap. 'One side's right.' 'No, the other side's right.' Nobody wants to see that. Make it a comedy, because it *is* funny. Tragic, of course, but funny.

Howard holds out some sheets of paper.

Howard I've written it all out for you here. You can use it if you like.

David M I can see everyone wants to say it's a story about greed and fear . . .

Financial Journalist It's greed, isn't it? It's pure greed.

Jon M It's greed, fear and complacency.

Harry People literally driven insane by greed.

Chair of Mortgage Lender Fear and greed drive capitalism. Capitalism works when greed and fear are in the correct balance. This time they got out of balance. Too much greed, not enough fear. Shocked, are you? Shocked? Prefer a different system, would you?

David M And everyone wants to make the bankers the villains. But are they really?

Howard The bankers weren't villains, they were just hamsters on the wheel.

Author Honestly, we're not going to get anywhere if you insist on writing the play for me. You have to give me the material, not the play.

David M Yes, I'm just struck by how difficult it is.

Author I know it's difficult.

David M I don't envy you. It really is very difficult.

Author I know it's difficult. I'll worry about that. You just tell me the story.

THREE

Myron Scholes, cheerful, humorous, is at a blackboard. He wears a plaid jacket, and striped shirt. He chalks up the famous equation where C equals S multiplied by N etc. At the same time Masa (pronounced Masha), dark-haired, authoritative, starts explaining to the Author. As she does, an Announcer identifies participants.

Masa There are two things you have to understand about banking. It's about leverage and it's about risk.

Announcer Masa Serdarevic. About to join the *Financial Times*.

Masa Do you have any idea what I'm talking about?

Author Not yet. I'm hoping to.

Masa Where do you keep your own money?

Author In the Post Office.

Masa OK.

He thinks a moment.

OK. In the Post Office?

Author Yes.

Announcer Paid by the National Theatre to explain finance to the author. Age twenty-three.

Masa I'm afraid I know nothing about the theatre.

Author It's fine. Really, it's fine.

7

Masa My brother goes. He's heard of you.

Author Good. Go ahead.

Masa So let's start with something simple. John Maynard Keynes. Keynes said that all innovations in finance are innovations in leverage. Crudely, leverage is what you borrow in proportion to what you've got. A bank takes your money and sets it to work.

Author I understand that.

Masa Banks pretend they're keeping your money, but they're not. They're lending it out, so they can make money for themselves. Now obviously when they lend money they're taking a risk. They take extra risk when they lend it to people who may or may not be able to pay it back – that's called sub-prime lending –

Author Ah yes. 'Sub-prime.' I've heard of that.

Masa It means lending to people who aren't reliable – people with irregular income, regular people, in fact. The other risk bankers take is when they perform any financial operation which depends on guessing what may happen in the future.

Author Isn't that what speculation is?

Masa Sure. But up until recently, although people were always coming up with ingenious systems, crackpot systems, nobody really believed mathematics could be used to predict the future. Then –

Masa turns towards the blackboard.

Announcer Myron Scholes. One-time academic and investment advisor.

Myron gestures at the blackboard.

Scholes All right, let's look at this, the Black–Scholes formula.

8

Masa Myron Scholes invented a formula.

Scholes It's perfectly simple. I can explain it to you without difficulty.

Masa Myron Scholes helped run a hedge fund in Greenwich, Connecticut. It was called Long Term Capital Management.

Author And a hedge fund is . . . ?

Masa A hedge fund is essentially an investment fund, aimed at professionals and licensed to use high-risk strategies. High risk, high return.

Author Go on.

Masa In 1973 Scholes and a fellow academic, Fisher Black, had come up with an algebraic formula for pricing options.

Author Tell me what an option is.

Masa OK. If a stock is worth a certain sum of money today, and I believe it'll be worth double that in six months' time, then it'll suit me to have the 'option' of buying it in six months at a price something less than what I believe it will become.

Author It's gambling.

Masa Yes. It's gambling.

Author Gambling on the future.

Masa So for the person selling, the crucial thing is to decide what fee to charge for the option. In the seventies, two Harvard academics – you'll notice it's a running theme, how many of the people who fucked up capitalism came from Harvard – some came from Harvard, some from Goldman Sachs, most came from both – anyway, they claimed that it was possible to use modern computing power to manage risk by mathematical means.

Scholes refers to the symbols he has drawn on the blackboard.

Scholes What we have here is the Black–Scholes formula. An option's value, C, depends on five variables. The current market price of the stock, S. The agreed future price for the option, X. The time till the expiry of the option, T. The risk-free interest rate, R. And the decisive factor – the expected fluctuation of the stock price, called volatility, and represented by the Greek letter sigma. By working to the following formula –

He demonstrates.

– C equals S multiplied by N brackets d one which is the area under the Normal curve at d one, minus, X multiplied by e to the power negative rT multiplied by N brackets d two which is the area under the normal curve at d two. d one equals, log of S over X plus, open brackets, r plus sigma squared over two, close brackets, multiplied by T, all divided by sigma times the square root of T. d two equals d one minus sigma times the square root of T, it is possible accurately to arrive at the optimum selling price for option contracts. Does anyone have any questions?

Masa In 1994 Scholes became a partner in a hedge fund which was so successful that it posted profits of first 43, then 41 per cent.

Author Can't argue with that.

Masa Scholes insisted that any portfolio which depended on his mathematical projections *must* be spread across as many positions as possible. Even if one or two went wrong, the laws of probability argued against everything going wrong at once. The fund borrowed massively, taking on huge leverage.

Author What does 'huge' mean?

Masa The ratio of borrowing to capital was sometimes as high as 50 to 1.

The man we know as George addresses us.

Soros Looking back it seems amazing to me that anyone imagined they could eliminate risk by mathematical models.

Announcer George Soros, one-time hedge-fund manager. Speculated against the pound in 1992.

Soros Even more shocking that anyone believed them when they did.

Announcer Today, global philanthropist and philosopher. Estimated net worth: eleven billion dollars.

Soros They really did think that everything was foreseeable. Myself, I was thirteen or fourteen when the Nazis arrived in Budapest. So I'm used to situations where things are far from equilibrium. My father had already taught me there are times when normal rules don't apply – to expect such times, to recognise them. As a kid my father had described to me how he had survived the Russian revolution – he had wonderful stories. The revolution was always real to me because I lived it through him. We knew there are times when nothing is normal and we knew how to cope with them. When the Germans came, our family survived, because we had the background. So no, I admit, I didn't believe them when they told me they could predict the future.

Masa In 1997 Myron Scholes was awarded the Nobel Prize in Economics.

Scholes acknowledges the applause of the Swedish Academy.

One year later, as a result of weaknesses in the Russian economy, Long Term Capital Management experienced losses which its computers had said were mathematically impossible. In four months, it was bust. In a Federal Court in 2004 Scholes' company was found guilty of tax evasion. The Black–Scholes model is still used to this day as the internationally recognised formula to calculate risk.

The Leading Industrialist begins to speak.

Industrialist You have to understand this is a world in which there is no past. People don't think about the past.

Announcer Leading industrialist, has headed up some of Britain's best-known companies. Reluctant to be identified.

Industrialist It's worse than that. They don't even know about the past. I was actually a banker for a couple of years, after the army and university. I went to work in a merchant bank, and you could feel the effect of the Great Depression, ingrained in bankers' minds. The mood hung over the place. There was a rule, repeated over and over. Debt one-third, equity two-thirds. Because that generation had an active memory. There was a cultural memory about what happens when risk gets out of control. And then that generation passed. The new generation has no memory. I've learnt not even to talk about the eighties, because nobody knows what I'm talking about. Thatcherism. Who remembers?

The man we know as Harry begins to speak.

Lovelock What happened in the last twenty years is that banks began to gamble with people's money in ways which nobody really understood.

Announcer Harry Lovelock, corporate lawyer. Has represented some of Britain's biggest companies in City mergers.

Lovelock It wasn't chance that banking became so complicated. Because the more complicated it becomes, the fewer people understand it. And that suits the bankers fine. Authority is bestowed on those who can maintain the mystique. Gambling is fine. I've nothing against gambling. With your own money. But when you begin to gamble with your customers' money, well that's a different thing, isn't it? That's when the ethical problems arise.

Announcer Myron Scholes was recently interviewed in an American newspaper about his life's work.

Deborah Solomon of the New York Times *appears.*

Solomon In retrospect is it fair to say that the idea that banks could manage risk was a total illusion?

Scholes What you're saying is negative. Life is positive too.

Solomon You're known as the intellectual father of the credit-default swap. Do you accept that label?

Scholes Let's see. If it's good, yes. If not, no.

Solomon Some economists believe that mathematical models like yours lulled banks into a false sense of security. I am wondering if you have revised your ideas.

Scholes smiles, happy.

Scholes I haven't changed my ideas.

FOUR

Music. The stage changes. Masa and the Author are joined by David Marsh.

Marsh To understand the history of what happened in this country, you have to understand the history of New Labour.

Masa I want you to meet David Marsh.

The Author shakes hands with Marsh.

Author Hello, David.

Marsh Hello, David.

Announcer David Marsh, Chairman of London and Oxford, Capital Markets plc.

Masa Used to work at the *Financial Times*.

Author Does everyone in this story work at the *Financial Times*?

Masa London School of Economics, Goldman Sachs, *Financial Times* – that covers just about everyone.

Marsh New Labour came to power determined to prove it was economically competent.

Author Sure.

Marsh They wanted to tackle the old accusation that Labour governments always end up bankrupt. To do that, they had to demonstrate they would be no threat to business, no threat to the City.

Lovelock returns.

Lovelock In the nineteenth century the City had been this huge enabler. It paid for railways in South America, for mines in South Africa. In the twentieth century Margaret Thatcher wanted to make it that again. Her masterstroke was to end exchange control, freeing up markets, de-regulating. So before he got into office Brown was looking for a masterstroke too. And he found it. Giving independence to the Bank of England.

Marsh In 1997 Brown and his good friend Balls had the idea of separating the Bank from government, and giving it just one target – the control of inflation.

Author So independence then has been a great success?

Marsh It's too soon to say. You can only judge these things in the long term. In fact, Mervyn King, who's

Governor of the Bank, always gets shirty when Germans boast the record of their Central Bank. Mervyn says, 'Hmm . . . well, if you take the hundred-year view, there is that embarrassing moment in 1923 when your inflation was at three trillion per cent. That does rather push your average up.'

Marsh laughs.

Lovelock Anyway as a kind of kicker to independence, Brown also decreed that regulation would no longer be the bank's responsibility. A new organisation, the Financial Services Authority –

Marsh The FSA –

Lovelock – was set up soon after, so the bank could concentrate purely on monetary policy.

Marsh People believe they got the idea of separating regulation from the famously enigmatic former Chairman of the Federal Reserve Board, Alan Greenspan.

Alan Greenspan, a lugubrious old cove, American, in his eighties, appears.

Announcer Alan Greenspan, winner of the Enron Award for Distinguished Public Service.

Greenspan If you think you understood me, it's because I mis-spoke.

Marsh Brown and Balls have this fascination with all things American, they worship America, so whatever Greenspan suggests, they do – there's your villain for you . . .

Author All right, all right . . .

Marsh Brown adored Greenspan, there's even a plaque to him in the Treasury, can you believe it?

They have been joined by a Young Man at the Bank, willowy, late twenties.

Young Man I certainly don't think Greenspan was responsible for the separation, I wouldn't think he was that involved in detail.

Announcer An employee at the Bank of England. Has to remain anonymous.

Young Man Though mind you, there is that ridiculous plaque in the Treasury.

Marsh It was the FSA who allowed the Royal Bank of Scotland to build up a level of debt over thirty times their equity. In the old days, the Bank of England would at least have raised an eyebrow. Have you heard that phrase? Eyebrow regulation?

Author No. No. I haven't.

Marsh Meaning: they would have looked at the balance sheet, called Fred Goodwin in and said, 'Steady on, old chap.'

Author And as they said it?

Marsh You got it. Raised an eyebrow.

Announcer Leading industrialist again.

Industrialist Things always go wrong, don't they? When you divide responsibility. If you split responsibility, it's only human nature to imagine the other person must have done it. You think, 'Oh, I'm not sure who's meant to be watching out for this, but I'm sure it's not me.'

Young Man The problem was, they couldn't find anyone to run the FSA. So the Deputy Governor had to go and do it.

The man identified as Howard comes on, bristling slightly.

Davies It's true. I didn't intend to be Chairman of the FSA.

Announcer Howard Davies. One-time Deputy Governor of the Bank of England, now Director of the London School of Economics.

Author So, the obvious question. Is it all your fault?

Davies No it fucking well isn't.

Author But people do blame you, don't they?

Davies I get a certain amount of blame and it does annoy me.

Author I'm sure.

Davies I do get annoyed.

Author I'm sure.

Davies Because the financial crisis is actually down to two things. It's down to derivatives and it's down to housing. I left the FSA in 2003. At that point credit default swaps, which have caused so much of the trouble, were running at around £3 trillion. At the time everything collapsed, they'd reached £63 trillion. So that's the order of difference. So I fucking well do get angry, yes. It didn't happen on my watch. If you ask the basic question, 'Did I sit there while this explosion was going on and did I miss it?' then the answer is no. But you can ask the subtler question, 'Did I create the faulty apparatus which led to this?'

Author May I?

Davies Ask it. By all means.

Author I'm new to all this, but surely it's you that created the idea of light-touch regulation?

Davies All right, but I don't like the phrase 'light-touch'.

Author OK.

Davies I always say to people, 'Please don't use it, it's not meaningful.'

Author OK.

Davies Because, honestly, either you regulate or you don't.

Author I see.

Davies It is the case that at the FSA we did believe in being co-operative. We saw ourselves as watchdogs, not as bloodhounds. That was a choice. That's the Davies defence. In fact, the analogy I use is with policing – we were neighbourhood police, not CID. The problem CID has is nobody will talk to them, because everyone knows they have to be careful what they say. Whereas people *will* talk to the neighbourhood police. You can have a sensible discussion. You can say, 'I've run over my neighbour's dog backing out of my garage.' And we will say, 'Well maybe you should go and tell the neighbour and offer to bury it.' And that way you can clear the thing up. Of course if you come to the police and say, 'I've run over my neighbour's child,' then that's a different thing.

Author Quite.

Davies In so far as 'light touch' means anything at all, it means that usually when an institution discovered it had made a mistake, it came to us and owned up. In the US, they're much heavier about these things. No one can go into a room without a lawyer. So tell me why it's them who ends up with crooks like Bernie Madoff and Alan Stanford.

Announcer Employee at the Bank of England, again.

Young Man The FSA was obsessed with the sale of products – what we call Conduct of Business, telling people things like, 'This advertisement is misleading.' But, you know, there's a second aspect to regulation and that's Prudential Supervision. That means having some regard for the overall health of the system. And that's the very thing that got overlooked.

Hammond Look, you're not going to tell me, nobody's going to tell me Gordon Brown was interested in regulation.

They have been joined by the man we know as Paul.

Announcer Paul Hammond, head-hunter for Hammond Partners, specialising in global search for financial personnel.

Hammond He didn't give a damn about regulation.

Author Didn't he? I thought he was meant to be a control freak.

Davies Gordon Brown was completely uninterested in regulation. He never made any criticism of anything we did.

Hammond Do you have any idea what happened to the financial sector while Gordon Brown was Chancellor? Do you?

Author Tell me.

Hammond It expanded to a point where it accounted for 9 per cent of the British economy. *Nine per cent.* It became Britain's very own Hong Kong. As British industry failed, it was replaced by British financial services. You see, London was ideally placed. It was in the right time zone. And we speak English. Just as Japan closes, London opens. And London is still open when New York opens. London became the financial capital of the world. The whole Labour government was predicated on the prosperity of the City. Not only was it 9 per cent of the

economy, but it generated 27 per cent of the tax take.
Can you imagine that figure? Do you want me to say it
again?

Author By all means.

Hammond The City was providing him with 27 per cent
of his taxes. It was his cash cow. Of course he wasn't
going to regulate it! Because with the money it made him
he could do all the things he was really interested in, like
schools and hospitals.

Marsh The thing about Brown you have to understand
is that he has no real love for the City. He's a Scottish
Presbyterian, so when the church fete comes round he's
happy to have it opened by the local bigwig, he'll let
them run the tombola, that's how he thinks of the
money-makers, but he doesn't have any feeling for them.
Brown was happy with the City as long as it generated
huge amounts of cash.

*Jon Cruddas MP arrives, dark-haired, forties,
triumphant.*

Cruddas Sixty quarters of growth!

Announcer Jon Cruddas MP.

Cruddas Sixty quarters of growth!

Announcer Stood for the Labour deputy leadership in
2007, seen as a future progressive candidate for leader.

Cruddas Think about that. The longest period of
uninterrupted growth for three hundred years. New
Labour bet the ranch on the financial services. And it
paid off. Tony Blair told us it was a new economy. The
old cycles of capitalism had been abolished. The class-
based solutions of old Labour were no longer relevant,
because the laws of political economy had been
suspended! It was a new society and only New Labour

understood it. You no longer had to worry about questions of distribution because you had growth. An end to history! The rise and fall of epochs is over.

He imitates Gordon Brown.

'An end to boom and bust!'

Davies It was this obsession with inflation, you see. Central banks and politicians thought everything was fine, everything must be fine because inflation was under control. In fact all these other things were going on in the economy but nobody was looking.

Young Man The whole system was regarded as perfect. And that did bother me very much.

Davies Meanwhile, over in the United States, Alan Greenspan was congratulating himself on having avoided the recession that might have followed on 9/11.

Greenspan You have to remember, people thought the world was going to end.

Davies So Greenspan engineered a boom. He unleashed a lot of cheap money and off we went. Party time.

Cruddas Brown was being acclaimed as the most successful Chancellor of all time. Only you know how the Roman conquerors had people beside them whispering '*Sic transit gloria*'. Gordon needed somebody whispering 'Regulate'.

Hammond He hadn't abolished boom and bust. He'd taken us on the biggest boom of all time. Now he'd be taking us through the biggest bust.

FIVE

Music. The stage changes once more. Masa and the Author are revealed.

Masa How are you getting on?

Author I'm fine. Really. I am. I'm fine.

Masa A glass of water?

Author No thank you.

Masa Because now I'm going to lead you to the sources of the great disaster. Are you ready?

Author I think I am.

Masa There are two basic triggers. One is sub-prime mortgages. The other is securitised credit arrangements.

Author Don't think you're losing me, because you're not.

Masa Good.

Author I'm going to stick with this.

Masa Good.

Author Are you going to use the word 'toxic'?

Masa I'm about to, yes.

Author Don't worry, I'm not panicking, I'm understanding. It may look like panic, but it's understanding.

Masa All right, I'm going to take this slowly.

Author No, no, no, whatever you do, don't take it slowly.

Masa Why not?

Author Because this is my area of expertise. You know about money, Masa, I know about rhetoric. If you take things slowly, nobody understands.

He separates each word for emphasis.

'Now – is the winter – of our – discontent – made – glorious – summer – by this – *son* – of York . . .'

He looks at Masa.

You see, your brain dies while it listens. It's not chance, the iambic pentameter has been scientifically proven to have the basic beat which corresponds to the speed of waves in the brain. Thus:

He does it again, at speed.

'Now is the winter of our discontent made glorious summer by this son of York.' Please, take it quickly.

Masa OK. Here we go.

Masa pauses, then starts.

The fetish of Anglo-Saxon capitalism is home ownership. You have to own your home. A house is not just a place to live, it's a chip in the casino. Because in order to buy it, the chances are, you borrow money. And once you've bought it, you have an asset.

Author In theory.

Masa And once you have that asset, hey, you can borrow more money. Now in the old days banks were rooted in communities. You knew your bank manager, his name was Martin or Philip, and he gave you your mortgage because he trusted you. In fact that's what the word 'credit' means. Trust.

Author It's a beautiful idea.

Masa It is.

Author Credit. Trust.

Masa But then suddenly mortgage brokers realised banks were now willing to buy up and pass on every mortgage loan they could issue. The business of lending on debt became huge and hugely profitable. And to test the quality of the mortgages, banks came to depend on professional rating agencies. Under pressure from the banks, those agencies became somewhat free with their ratings. Mysteriously, everything got rated AAA. Because the freer the rating agencies were, the more the banks were able to lend. At the same time Alan Greenspan said something rather revealing.

Greenspan appears.

Greenspan 'In a market economy based on property rights it is critical to have as broad a swathe of people as possible with a vested interest in making that system work.'

Masa And George Bush then said, 'We want everyone in America to own their own home.' After that, the criterion for a loan became, 'Can you breathe? If you can breathe we'll give you a loan.'

Scott Rudmann appears, an American in his forties, in blue jeans and blazer.

Rudmann I began to notice something was happening when I went back to California.

Announcer Scott Rudmann, founder of a private equity group, Nectar Capital.

Author What was that?

Rudmann It was very strange.

Announcer Educated at Harvard.

Rudmann All my friends had become mortgage brokers. I thought this is odd, how many mortgage brokers can there be in any one town? And they were handing out million-dollar mortgages to people they called Ninjas. You know?

Author No Income, No Job, No Assets.

Rudmann That's it. And I thought, hang on, this has happened before. It happened with Savings and Loans. The Savings and Loans scandal. In the eighties. It shook me because this was a repeat. And nobody seemed to remember the consequences.

Announcer David Marsh again.

Marsh At one point there were a million mortgage brokers in the US and when you went to them and said, 'I can't pay my mortgage,' they'd say, 'Don't worry, we'll give you a bigger one and that'll fix the problem.'

Masa And now because the banks were taking on so much debt, they looked for a way of offsetting the risk associated with that debt. And they came up with this idea called securitised credit arrangements.

Author Ah, now we get to it.

Masa What they mean is: rather than take the whole debt yourself, rather than hold on to it, you cut it into pieces and sell it on in packages. You take some of mine, I'll take some of yours.

Marsh It's called slicing and dicing.

Masa And in ten years this method of dealing with debt – dividing it up and selling it on in packages – grew out of all recognition. Everybody took everybody's else's. You take a package but you don't necessarily look to see what's in it. Because in theory it's an asset. On the balance sheet, what you've got is an asset. And what can you do with an asset? You can use it to borrow more.

Marsh What you can say quite clearly is that the invention of these new instruments made certain things possible which would not otherwise have been possible. A huge amount of money began to wash around the world. And the bankers were willing to provide money for all of us who wished to live beyond our means. All of us.

Rudmann Consumer debt, credit card debt, mortgage debt: any kind of debt you could get into, we got into. The US and the UK went from being nations of producers to being nations of borrowers.

Marsh Everything was possible. Why? Because the bankers had come up with the facility, the *means* for us all to have more money than we earned.

Author And that means was securitised credit arrangements?

The Leading Industrialist is back.

Announcer Leading industrialist again.

Industrialist These securitised credit arrangements were a new invention, and they engendered a new level of hubris. They were so profitable that they made people believe, 'Oh, we've found a new answer to risk.' But they hadn't. Interesting, actually. The very opposite. They'd made risk worse.

Marsh smiles, rueful.

Marsh You know, there's this phrase Giscard d'Estaing picked up about the 'exorbitant privilege' of the US. Have you heard that phrase?

Author No.

Marsh 'Exorbitant privilege.' George Bush was happy to run up bigger and bigger national debts. Because it was understood the US was a kind of historical exception.

Author It was too big to fail?

Marsh That's right.

Author The rules didn't apply?

Marsh That's right.

Author Not to the US?

Marsh It couldn't fail because if the US failed, everything would fail. Traditionally US governments had sought to balance the books like everyone else, but suddenly under Bush the US was borrowing five billion dollars a day, because he wanted to invade various parts of the world. Bush had a rather pricey foreign policy.

Young Man Bush really did believe the rules don't apply to America. The paradox is that when the crash comes, everyone runs to the dollar for safety. It's crazy. Investors rush to the very place that unleashed the chaos.

Rudmann laughs.

Rudmann You do have to admire the guys on Wall Street. You really do. Every so often they come up with these incredible products. Securitisation? It's only a version of junk bonds. Hello? Does nobody remember Michael Milken? Milken was a sort of genius who bundled up junky bonds, devised a mathematical model and said, 'Look, the rate of default can be calculated mathematically. Take a bundle of bonds – sure, some of them will default, but most won't, and I can prove by pure math you're not going to lose.'

Marsh The reason securitisation is so dangerous is because in a normal market, when someone defaults it's the lender who feels the pain. If it's your fault, it's you who pays. As in life.

Author You're right.

Marsh Because the person who originates the loan is also the person who holds it.

Author Same person.

Marsh Yes. But once the originator and the holder become separated, then the pain moves around, and it moves in disguise, if you like. You stub your toe but it's your elbow which hurts. Another way of putting it: the US exported their problems to the rest of the world.

David Freud, earlier identified as David F, comes on.

Freud Now Iceland's very interesting . . .

Announcer David Freud, banker and privatisation expert; floated British Airways, floated British Steel, floated Eurotunnel.

Freud It's actually such an interesting story.

Author Why?

Announcer Ex-*Financial Times*.

Freud I had a friend who tried to find out why so many banks were now in Iceland, of all places. Iceland, which had no banks, suddenly had a lot.

Author It was strange, I remember, everyone started talking about Iceland.

Freud It turns out there were five friends who lived on the same fjord. And one of these friends thought: what's the one essential thing you need for a business? You need leverage. And so he worked out the rules. One: if you want leverage, borrow. Two: if you want real leverage, buy a bank. Three: if you want real, real leverage, buy an investment bank. Because if you have an investment bank, you can borrow as much as you like. And so one of these businessmen bought a bank, to get himself leverage. And all his friends on that fjord thought, I'm not letting him have that advantage, so they bought banks as well. And suddenly there were five investment banks in Iceland. And that's why the whole country's bankrupt today. And that's it, you see, when a bubble happens, you don't look at the whole picture, you just look at the person next to you, the man on the same fjord, and you think, 'He's making money, why can't I?'

Author I'm sorry.

Freud What?

Author I'm listening to this stuff, I've been listening to it for weeks, and I pretend to understand, but I don't.

Freud What don't you understand?

Author All over the world interest rates are at what – 4 per cent, 5 per cent? Then some Icelandic banks appear and they offer 10 per cent. Does nobody think, '*How is that possible?*'

Freud Ah.

Author Is it really possible that in Iceland bankers are 5 per cent cleverer than bankers in the rest of the world? Is that possible? Does nobody think, 'Stinking fish!' Because, sorry, look, I know you'll say it's all Harry Hindsight, but it's what I'd think.

Freud If someone offered you 10 per cent?

Author Stinking fish! And then Bernie Madoff offers you 15 per cent. 15 per cent? Year on year? Stinking fish!

Freud Yes, but if you're managing a pension fund, and interest rates are low and people say to you, 'I know a place where you can get more,' it's very hard to say, 'No thank you, I'm happier with less.' Hard to say that. People start thinking you must be stupid.

Rudmann You don't get it! Once you're in a bubble, it needs nerves of steel to stay out. Can you imagine the pressure? On any trader? Everyone around you is making money, and they do it with securitised credit arrangements. And you're the one who says 'I don't believe in securitised credit arrangements'? *Get out of here!*

Ronald Cohen comes on, silvery, elegant.

Cohen The way I put it is to say that a bubble is always a good idea in which intelligent people invest, and then stupid people follow.

Announcer Sir Ronald Cohen, Britain's pioneer of venture capitalism, first inductee into the Private Equity Hall of Fame.

Cohen The intelligent people get out, while the stupid people redouble their efforts. Securitised credit arrangements were a perfectly intelligent idea, there's nothing wrong with them as such. There really isn't. But they do depend on debts being correctly rated. A great chunk of these securities were not correctly rated. If the ratings had been reliable, then the system would have worked.

George Soros returns.

Announcer George Soros again.

Soros In 1996 Greenspan made a famous speech warning against bubbles. And people praised him for it. He was saying that bubbles were irrational exuberance. But he got that wrong. They're not irrational. When I see a bubble coming, I'm thrilled. I participate. I buy the stock. You buy the stock when you see the bubble. I don't call that irrational, I call it highly rational. It's how I made my money.

Soros smiles and goes.

Cohen You know Greenspan made that famous speech in 1996, condemning irrational exuberance. But what's far more interesting is the speech he *didn't* make.

Author What speech was that?

Cohen In 2004 he didn't make a speech condemning a gargantuan appetite for risk. Because that's the speech he should have made and never did.

Author I like that phrase. Whose is it?

Cohen It's mine, actually.

Author 'Gargantuan appetite.' Hmm.

Cohen People were buying planes with debt, they were buying houses with debt, they were buying art with debt, they were buying everything with debt. Greenspan believed that it was the market which regulates. If you take a bad decision, the market punishes you. As far as Greenspan was concerned, that's regulation. But in fact it turns out that on a rising market you can be rewarded for bad decisions.

Freud There was a seventeen-year boom, and during that boom anyone who wanted to stay conservative didn't do well. It was Darwinian. The more money you make, the longer you survive. In our business if you make a fortune you're a genius. If you don't make a fortune, you're stupid. That's how it was. And everyone was fooled by the fact that the boom lasted so long – not six years, which is normal, or ten, which is also normal – this one lasted seventeen. Why? The real reason? Because people in China were working for 46 cents an hour, that's why. And so inflation was kept artificially low, because all these cheap goods flooded onto the market. They were working for us, for nothing. China's eighth biggest trading partner was Wal-Mart. All you had to do to make money was be in the right place at the right time. You punted and every time you punted you won. In fact after a lifetime in the City I've met an awful lot of leading businessmen and at the end I've concluded that there's no such thing as a genius entrepreneur.

Freud roars with laughter.

Author Or banker?

Freud Or banker. It's all just luck.

Paul Hammond returns.

Announcer Paul Hammond again.

Hammond There's a great saying in our profession. 'Never confuse genius with a bull market.' You may have made a lot of money but you'll be very foolish if you imagine it has anything to do with your talent. When the market's rising anyone can make money.

Cohen Look, if you're an intelligent banker, then when it's crazy, you know it's crazy. Of course you know. In your heart. Of course. But that doesn't stop you selling. Even though you may be feeling, 'This is going to end in tears.' So why don't you stop? Because markets have only one rule.

Author And that is?

Cohen *Caveat emptor.* Buyer beware! That is the rule. *Caveat emptor* is the confession which relieves you from guilt. If you design a product and it's stupid, then the buyer must be the judge. You are not trying to take people in. You are saying, 'Take it or leave it.' At the end of the day, your conscience is clear.

Adair Turner comes on, tall, with a shock of white hair, fifties.

Turner You mustn't start thinking of this as a conspiracy.

Announcer Adair Turner, ex-London School of Economics, became Chair of the FSA one week before the crash.

Turner You mustn't confuse accident with conspiracy.

Masa That's what I've been telling him! I keep trying to tell him that. He doesn't *listen*.

Turner Bankers didn't sit there saying, 'Let's fool people into securitised credit arrangements.' They sat there saying, 'Securitised credit arrangements, complex structured credits and credit derivatives – CDOs and CDO squareds – are a marvellous way of reducing risk.' They thought, oh, it's a wonderful thing if when a house-buyer in Indiana borrows money from the bank, the bank in Indiana doesn't have to carry that debt. It can be carried by a bank on the other side of the world. Bankers convinced themselves these innovations would make the system safer. This isn't a story about bankers fooling you. It's a story about bankers fooling themselves.

Author But I don't get it.

Turner Why not? Why don't you get it?

Author Because surely you have to deal with the fact that nobody understood these things.

Turner Didn't they?

Author *Nobody understood them.* Even Alan Greenspan, Chairman of the Federal Reserve, dear old Greenspan – he didn't understand them.

Turner Did he say that?

Author He said he had hundreds of people with PhDs working for him and they didn't understand them either. Wasn't it irresponsible of him to let these things exist if he didn't even understand them himself?

Turner Not if you have Greenspan's faith. Given his own principles his position is perfectly sensible. Greenspan's a believer in markets, the wisdom of the market. If professionally competent people make deals in their own self-interest, they'll come up with products and contracts which by definition are likely to make sense. And he also believes those arrangements work better when he keeps out of the way. He's like someone who rides in a Mercedes, he doesn't actually have to understand how the engine works. He's happy to delegate the smooth running of the machine to the mechanics. He has a certain confidence level that the Mercedes will always run well because in his experience it always has. But applied to financial markets that's a very dangerous assumption, because you can test drive a new car, but unfortunately you can't test drive a new financial system.

Lovelock returns.

Announcer Harry Lovelock again.

Lovelock If you look at what happened to the building societies, it's a terrible story.

Author Ah yes, the building societies.

Lovelock As an old puritan I loved the building societies because they represented such a wonderful notion of self-help.

Author Wonderful.

Lovelock They were essentially mutual saving societies which existed to help people buy houses. They served a social purpose. They were careful, they were frugal and they grew. Then one day the City comes along, it looks at the Halifax with its twelve million customers or whatever and it says, 'My God! What a great list of people.' And they think: What a shame that under building society rules you can't disclose that list, you can't sell them any

34

other products like pensions or life insurance. So everyone thinks, hey, why don't we turn this building society into a bank and then we can sell the customers all sorts of things, and we can grow exponentially.

As it happens I was working for the Bradford and Bingley, which was run by a group of very decent, very sound Yorkshiremen, who all said, 'We want to go on doing what we're doing. We want to lend money to people to help them buy houses.' But at the annual general meeting, some member put down a resolution saying 'Let's be a bank'. The board were left with no option but to obey.

Author Are you saying you had misgivings?

Lovelock I'm a lawyer. A lawyer has to do a lot of things he doesn't approve of. The members were after the windfall, that's what they wanted – a few thousand pounds. And yet the absurd thing is, most of them got that windfall in the form of shares, which they didn't even bother to cash, so that when the resulting bank went bust, they lost everything.

Once Bradford and Bingley became a bank, I remember taking an immediate dislike to a new non-exec who said, 'I want one thing from this company.' He said, 'What I want is regular, incremental growth.' In other words, he was saying, '*This company must grow every year.*'

Now we all know that nothing in the world shows regular incremental growth. You know that. I know that. But in the stock market they rip out the profit and bugger the future. The majority of investment isn't handled by individual investors – who can be bothered to look in the paper every day to see how their shares are doing? No, it's handled by fund managers, who are driven by quarterly figures. Every quarter, they have to prove they're doing better than other fund managers or else the client will take their money away. So fund managers are looking at businesses and demanding more and more money out of them.

I mean, there came a moment when you could smell the corruption. This was madness. If you said to a taxi driver, how would you like it to be a condition of driving your taxi that each year you pick up more fares than the year before, he would tell you you were off your head. And yet the people who engineered this madness – people who lent 125 per cent of the value of a house – refuse to admit they did anything wrong.

If I tell you the HBOS accounts run for 200 pages . . . and 28 of these pages are about corporate governance – oh yes, the remuneration committee has sat, the correct number of women have been appointed, the appropriate checks and balances are in place. It's all box-ticking. It's like a ship which you're being told is in apple-pie order, the decks are cleaned, the metal is burnished, the only thing nobody mentions, it's being driven at full speed towards an iceberg.

Soros returns.

Announcer Soros again.

Soros The financial crisis is a big blow to Britain, because financial institutions loom so large in the British economy. Do you have any idea of the scale of the thing?

Author I'm not sure I do.

Soros Judged by its assets, the Royal Bank of Scotland is the biggest company in the world. Did you know that?

Author I have to admit I didn't.

Soros At the time of its collapse, the Royal Bank of Scotland had assets of 1,900 billion pounds. The gross national product of your country was only 1,500 billion. In other words, RBS was bigger than the entire annual output of the British economy.

Author Blimey.

Soros And that's just one bank. You're always going to be in trouble when your banking sector is bigger than your entire economy. Don't get me wrong. Personally I like Britain. I love the British, I love their history, Bloomsbury, Cambridge, I see these things as high-points of civilisation. The way I put it is this: an imperial power in its last throes is always the pleasantest place to live.

Announcer Scott Rudmann again.

Rudmann I've worked in finance a long time and I believe if someone says to you, 'You are going to make 11 per cent to 20 per cent, and you're going to make it every year,' then you know something is deeply wrong. I don't care who tells you that. Whether it's Bernie Madoff, or a bank in Iceland. But I'm not sure regulation is going to help much, because regulators are not by definition the most financially talented people. What sort of person embarks on a career in finance and says, 'I want to be chief regulator'? The Finance Minister should get some of the blame because he's the one who's meant to look at the accounts. He's meant to have enough knowledge and skill to look at what's going on and say, 'Uh-oh, man, there's vapour all over the balance sheet.'

The man identified as Jon M comes on – Jon Moulton, Northern, fizzy, contemptuous. He is holding a fistful of paper.

Moulton Look at this Barclays balance sheet . . .

Announcer Jon Moulton . . .

Moulton Take a look at this!

Announcer Founder of Alchemy private equity, specialists in financial services and distressed debt.

Moulton smacks the papers with his hand.

Moulton 'Unobservable profit' – there it is. What the hell is it? I don't know. What responsible Chairman reading his own balance sheet would allow that to go out? But he hasn't read it, has he?

Author Hasn't he?

Moulton 'Vanilla products' – 'exotic products'. I'm a trainspotter and even I don't understand this.

He reads from the sheet.

It says here: 'Vanilla products are valued using Black–Scholes models, however some of the inputs are not observable.' Can anyone understand a word of that? *Non-observable inputs?* A non-observable input is about as much use as a virtual woman. Best one ever was an AIG balance sheet which announced, 'We have used the binomial expansion technique,' then said – and I promise you I am not making this up – 'We have added in Monte Carlo simulations when calculating the value of Super Senior credit default swaps.' As if Monte Carlo simulations would inspire confidence in the ordinary person! Oh and by the way, AIG will lose 160 billion dollars on these things. And they didn't even know they were there.

Cohen Someone must have mentioned Chuck Prince?

Author Nobody.

Announcer Ronald Cohen again.

Cohen Chuck Prince was Head of Citibank. He said, 'As long as the music is playing, you've got to get up and dance.' Wonderful, isn't it? The banks were all in a dancing marathon. You couldn't take a break, you had to keep dancing, and your only hope was that you'd be nearest the exit when the music stopped. You don't dare stop, because then your clients will remove their money and take it to another bank which is still dancing. And meanwhile the building is falling down, the roof is open to the sky, the hall's slipping off the pier and no one has the wit to stop the marathon.

Hammond There was always this problem with securitised credit arrangements. You've got these assets. At least, they're on your balance sheet. There are all these things you've bought, and you say they're assets. But in fact you don't know what they are. And so there comes this moment, doesn't there? There comes a tipping point. If you don't believe your own balance sheet, how can you believe other people's?

There is a silence.

Author Credit. Trust.

Hammond Precisely.

It's quiet. Jon Cruddas reappears silently.

Cruddas You see, I think it's the end of liberal economics. This is the end of the experiment.

Announcer Jon Cruddas again.

Cruddas I have this friend, you may know him, fought in the Spanish Civil War, was there at the Norway Debate when Chamberlain fell, friend of Nye Bevan's, and I asked him 'Do you know? Do you *know*? When you're living through great epochal change? Are you aware?'

Author You think it's a historic time?

Cruddas Interesting man, Tony Blair. He really is. He doesn't believe in history. Doesn't think it matters. Doesn't think it exists. And sometimes that's a good thing. He goes into Northern Ireland, pretends there's no history, just treats it as a problem, sitting there, waiting to be solved. And know what? It works. With his extraordinary lawyer's gifts, Blair solves it. But then he says there's no Labour Movement, there's no Labour history, there's no class struggle, in fact there's no such thing as class any more. There's only tribe. The tribe of politics, the tribe of finance. Has anyone begun to think through the implications of that? Do we really want tribe replacing class?

Another silence. The Author thinks a moment.

Author I'll tell you what puzzles me.

Cruddas Yes?

Author All those bankers . . .

Cruddas Oh sure . . .

Author Bankers encouraging debt, building up debt and not looking at their own balance sheets to see what's happening.

Cruddas Oh I understand that.

Author Do you?

Cruddas Sure.

Author Then tell me.

Cruddas I mean, come on. I think we can say if you're paid twenty million pounds a year, you're not incentivised to read your own accounts.

SIX

Music. The stage changes. Old familiars return: Davies, Freud, the Young Man at the Bank, Cohen.

Masa All right, you OK?

Author I'm fine.

Masa Any questions?

Author Yes. How do you know all this?

Masa I just know it.

Author Have you always known this stuff? Does everyone you know know this stuff?

Masa nods: 'Afraid so.'

Wow!

They both smile.

Wow!

Masa All right, let's get back to the story.

Author Let's.

Masa June 27th 2007. After ten happy years as Chancellor, Gordon Brown ascends to become Prime Minister.

Davies I do think he's culpable. Yes I do.

Announcer Howard Davies again.

Davies Just before he became Prime Minister, Brown delivered a completely irresponsible budget, cutting tax, stoking the boom, all so he could plan an election that never happened.

Freud You say Gordon Brown is clever. I don't think he's clever.

Announcer David Freud again.

Freud Because just when he needed to slow the economy down he pumped it up, doing what he calls 'investing in public services'. It makes me laugh when politicians talk about investing. Any spending you approve of you call 'investing'. And it was him who invented this disastrous target culture – control and command. Middle managers ticking boxes.

Author You really don't like him, do you?

Freud I went to Cambodia – now that was a target-driven culture, and it ended up with everyone starving.

Masa Just five days before Brown becomes Prime Minister the first tree falls in the forest. In the US, the investment bank Bear Stearns provides a 3.2 billion dollar loan trying unsuccessfully to bail out one of its own struggling hedge funds.

Davies I teach a course in the financial meltdown and it goes as follows:

> *The blackboard has appeared again and Davies is scrawling in chalk.*

S-L-U-M-P. Call it an acronym, call it a mnemonic. Whichever, it spells SLUMP and it's a drama in five acts.

> *He has written out the words:* 'SUB-PRIME, LIQUIDITY, UNRAVELLING, MELTDOWN, PUMPING'.

Act One. Sub-prime. It's never occurred to banks that the housing market might one day collapse. Well, right now it does. So this leads pretty quickly to Act Two. Liquidity. We can actually name the day when circulation stops. August 9th 2007. Banks don't know what exotic stuff they've got – just as important, they don't know what each other have got, and there's only one safe thing to do. Stop lending. Suddenly it's Cluedo. All the banks are looking at each other and thinking, now who is holding the bad stuff? The system freezes.

Cohen That's the problem with mathematical modelling.

Announcer Ronald Cohen again.

Cohen When you model risk, you only model your own risk. You don't model for the whole system. Banks were only interested in their own position. At no point did any bank ask, 'What will happen if *no one* can borrow and *no one* can lend?' That was outside the model.

Turner comes back.

Announcer Adair Turner again.

Turner Nobody understood how risky the whole system had become. And that's the answer to the Queen's question.

Author The Queen?

Turner Yes. The Queen went to the London School of Economics . . .

Author The Queen did?

Turner And she asked them, 'Why did nobody see it coming?' And the answer is: because there was a collective failure to see how all the bits of the system fitted together. No one thought it was their job to look at the whole picture. The FSA didn't think it was their job. The Bank of England didn't think it was theirs. And if, say, you were on the board of a bank, and you saw all these complex products and contracts on the balance sheet, and you called in the risk manager and he said, 'It's all right, we can carry this amount of risk, and here's how,' then in a way you'd discharged your duty. Because you didn't go on to ask, 'And are all banks in the same position as us? Are all financial institutions carrying these kinds of risks? And what is the collective effect of that? What if all the banks try to sell these assets simultaneously?'

David Freud returns.

Announcer David Freud again.

43

Freud That's the drawback with statistics. The odds against a man one-and-a-half foot tall coming into this room are very, very high. But if he comes through that door, then it doesn't really matter, does it, what the odds were? You've still got an eighteen-inch man to deal with.

Masa Events that models had predicted would happen once in ten thousand years happened every day for three days. And in Britain, thirty-four days later, we had our first casualty. It was called Northern Rock.

The Young Man at the Bank starts laughing.

Young Man Northern Rock, my God! Now that was quite a weekend. What a weekend! Panic at the Bank as Northern Rock goes down.

A Journalist from the Northern Echo *comes on, forties, abrasive.*

Journalist There was something tragically provincial about the whole thing, wasn't there?

Author Tell me what you mean by that.

Announcer Journalist. *Northern Echo.* Prefers not to be named.

Journalist I'm not the first person to point out this wasn't actually a British banking crisis.

Author What do you mean?

Journalist Come on, this was a Scottish banking crisis. HBOS and RBS, they were both Scottish. The Prime Minister was Scottish, the Chancellor Alistair Darling was Scottish, and Northern Rock – where are we? Newcastle! As near to Scotland as makes no difference . . .

Author That doesn't make it provincial.

Journalist No, no, I don't mean that, I mean, the way the whole thing was like a *Carry On* film.

Author What was?

Journalist Northern Rock! You must have noticed, you could hardly miss it, Northern Rock was run by this ludicrous man called Adam Applegarth, with this enormous head . . .

The Journalist puts his hands round his own head to demonstrate.

Big head, bald head, pointy head, and he had this woman, remember? He had a mistress in the bank and she looked like Cruella De Vil, and oh, he had to have his holidays at certain times, went nuts when his diary got changed, because secretly he was off with this woman – Amanda Smithson her name – and inevitably in the way of things, she became known as Randy Mandy, and there were Moulin Rouge-themed parties, attended by five hundred and twenty-five what were called Northern Rockers. There were anonymous letters to Applegarth's wife, and the whole thing seemed *News of the World*. Very British and very *News of the World*. Except it wasn't. It was people's lives, it was their lifelong saving . . .

The Author turns to the Young Man at the Bank.

Author How was it at the Bank if England?

Young Man Oh, unbelievable! It was unbelievable!

Author In what way?

Young Man We should have known we were in trouble because we'd all been preparing for a two-day seminar called 'The Great Stability'. Exactly! You couldn't make it up. A bunch of academics gathering to celebrate the success of British monetary policy. And the opening-night dinner was just a fest of complacency. Then somebody lent in to the Governor's ear. 'Northern Rock's all over the ten o'clock news . . .'

Paul Mason comes on, stocky, in his forties.

Mason If there's an image of the crisis that's going to last for ever, it's people standing trying to get their money out of Northern Rock.

Announcer Paul Mason, economics editor, *Newsnight*.

Mason On August 9th, Mervyn King had said there was no crisis. By September 14th he had a full-scale run on a British bank.

Young Man The minute we knew, we should have guaranteed people's money. But we had no idea people were going to stand in the street. We should have known: in Britain when people see a queue they join it.

Mason As a journalist, if you deal with King, he can be quite fussy. Quite fussy and quite academic. At press conferences, King will correct your questions, saying things like, 'It isn't called the base rate, it's called the bank rate.'

Young Man Mervyn's a very cultivated man, he likes music and cricket. He's a word man, not a body-language man, he speaks in the most beautiful well-formed paragraphs, he's far more urbane and civilised than Gordon Brown, but in one way they're alike: they share a horror of making their minds up in open debate. If you really want to know, I'd say Mervyn is not a man who reacts well to the unexpected. If you travel with him, it can be quite alarming. Alarming! If the car isn't there or the train is late . . . he panics.

Mason In the past if the Chancellor said your money was safe, then your money was safe. But Monday came and there were still queues in the street. After four days of panic I was at a press conference and I said, 'Chancellor, the problem is when you say everything's going to be fine, nobody believes you.' And at that point Alistair Darling was forced to spell out that he was standing by every penny in Northern Rock's bank accounts. And you could see his team go white. And when afterwards we all asked, 'What power does he have? What statutory basis? Is he planning to introduce legislation?' they replied, 'It is at the word of the Chancellor. For three hundred years the word of the Chancellor has been good.' I don't know why they chose three. They could have chosen any number really.

Journalist What I loved best was that Alistair Darling's own mortgage was with Northern Rock. In the North East we were quite proud of that. And I also loved that the FSA had recently rated Northern Rock. It was providing one mortgage in five in the UK, it was growing at 15 per cent, its lending had quadrupled from £25 billion to £100 billion, and it was rated 'low-risk'.

The Chair of a Mortgage Lender comes on, white-haired, distinguished.

Chair of Mortgage Lender You see, mine's a strange story because my whole life I'd been reasonably successful in what used to be called merchant banking.

Announcer The former chair of a mortgage lender. Unwilling to be identified.

Chair of Mortgage Lender And at fifty-five I realised I was fagged out, it was time to retire, because fifty-five doesn't understand thirty-five. I'd lost touch. Apart from anything, the young nowadays want to be assessed all the time. They want to be told how they're doing. Do you want that?

Author Not in the slightest.

Chair of Mortgage Lender Me neither. But it's a different generation, isn't it? It's everywhere. 'How am I doing?' they keep saying, and they want an answer. It's manager of the month. It's gong-shows. It's *Big Brother*. Roll of drums. 'And the winner is . . .' I don't pretend to understand it. Anyway, I retire, confused. Then someone asks me to be chairman of a mortgage lender. And I think, 'All right, I've done action jobs all my life, now's the time to do a wisdom job.'

I have to make one basic point. Banks only ever go bust because they run out of money. They don't go bust for any other reason. They don't go bust because they make bad loans. They don't go bust because they sell securitised credit arrangements. They go bust because there is no money. That's the only reason.

So, August 2007. A cloud no bigger than a man's hand. There's some sort of liquidity crisis. The biggest market in the world is liquidity: banks lending to banks. They do it in the belief they'll get it back. When that belief goes, they cease to lend. That was August 2007, and so in the twelve months following – and here I'm summarising the most painful time of my life – given what happened elsewhere in the system, we were ultimately too small to survive. It took about a year. But in the end we turned out to be too small.

Author You went down like Northern Rock?

Chair of Mortgage Lender Yes, but we were not aggressive like Northern Rock.

Author What does 'aggressive' mean?

Chair of Mortgage Lender Oh come on, you know perfectly well. Northern Rock had ways of accounting. But we were honest. I've got to do my legs.

Author Please.

The Chair gets up and shakes his legs.

Chair of Mortgage Lender I've been through these events in my head. Over and over. Horrid self-doubt. Horrid,

horrid, horrid. I've made a responsible living. My whole life. Then I become chairman of a mortgage lender and it goes plop. And I ask myself: have I lost my judgement? Have I been blinded by clever, evil people? People say banks went bankrupt because the boards were remiss, because they didn't understand what their own executives were doing. Well, my board was packed with experienced business people. These were not nodding donkeys. Nor were they renegade, cowboy characters. Or else we get hot under our little British collars and say the Yanks corrupted us. But one of the things no one likes to point out is that the consumer got a great deal. The banks got more and more competitive. They offered better and better deals. Northern Rock was the darling of the Stock Exchange. And we were the boring old plodder. People said, 'Why can't you be more like Northern Rock?' But it made no difference. This was a tsunami. Good and bad, we all drowned in the tsunami.

Young Man Even after we'd moved in and nationalised Northern Rock, nobody really clocked how big a deal it was going to be. People said, 'It's another storm in a wok.' Nobody said 'OK, this is the big one.'

SEVEN

Music. The stage changes. Davies goes back to his blackboard.

Masa All right, how you doing?

Author I'm holding in there.

Masa Good, because you've gone a funny colour. What is that?

Author I think it's the blood draining from my body.

Masa I see. OK.

Author Take no notice. Tell me about the big one.

Masa The big one was Lehman Brothers.

Davies points at his blackboard.

Davies So, let's run this back. Let's start from what I call the Unravelling. In the UK Mervyn King and the government enter a rather disorderly passage, trying to do ridiculous things like sell Northern Rock to Richard Branson . . .

Author I must say, the moment you hear the words 'Richard Branson' . . .

Davies Precisely. Deeply embarrassing. And then for a year after that, you have a nervous period, as in Shakespeare, when nobody knows what's going to happen.

Author Yes. That's always Act Three.

Davies You're right. Act Three. Nine months, a year goes by, things aren't good but it isn't yet the catastrophe.

A Hedge Fund Manager comes on. He's American, personable, early fifties.

Hedge Fund Manager All our problems were down to the Wall Street securitisation industry.

Announcer American hedge fund manager. Life-long professional and Wall Street insider.

Hedge Fund Manager And be clear – this is an industry I know very well. Wall Street pooled bad assets, packaged them in opaque structures, and sold them to investors. And when these investments began to fall, they didn't fall a few per cent, or 10 per cent, they fell 40, 50, 80 per cent.

Davies It's safe to say that if the US Treasury had had any idea of what would happen when they let Lehman go down they wouldn't have done it. It should have been quietly managed out of existence. Instead –

Hedge Fund Manager Lehman had been in trouble a long time because people felt it wasn't transparent. Its CEO, Erin Callan, had promised she was happy to open the kimono and let everyone see the story. But I guess the Fed felt the kimono was still in place.

Author Is that why they let Lehman go?

Hedge Fund Manager That, and. You can't help noticing, Lehman's rivals on Wall Street weren't too unhappy with the decision. After all, Hank Paulson was the US Treasury Secretary. He'd worked at Goldman Sachs. There was a long history of involvement between Goldman Sachs and the US Treasury.

Author What are you saying? I don't quite know what you're saying.

Hedge Fund Manager Let's spell it out: nobody believes the US Treasury would have let Goldman Sachs go down.

The Young Man at the Bank returns.

Young Man Lehman could easily have saved itself, that's what everyone forgets. It had a perfectly good offer from the Korea Development Bank. It was sheer arrogance that they insisted on going to the US government instead.

Hedge Fund Manager The Treasury had just saved Fannie Mae and Freddie Mac, they knew Merrill Lynch was having difficulties, they had AIG to deal with . . .

Davies You couldn't let AIG go, because it was so involved in China, and if the Chinese economic system was disrupted, then you were really in trouble.

Hedge Fund Manager So they loaded the gun, pointed it at Lehman and pulled the trigger. Bang! It was the biggest corporate failure in history.

Davies Panic.

Young Man The Fed decided to draw a line in the sand, and unfortunately it was the wrong line, with catastrophic consequences.

Hedge Fund Manager They were trying to teach Lehman a lesson. Boy! Boy! Did they get that wrong! People were waking up all over the world, in Tokyo, in Zurich, screaming at the Fed 'Wrong! Wrong decision!'

Young Man You were watching meltdown, like a supernova exploding.

Davies chalks on the board.

Davies Act Four. Meltdown. Meltdown arrives once we hit what's called 'the innocent bystander' test.

Author What is that test?

Davies If you have a bank called the Hare Bank and it's private, then it can be allowed to collapse, because it exists to service professional investors who are meant to understand risk. But if the Hare Bank has everyday clients, clients with current accounts, then innocent bystanders are getting hurt and that's different. The Fed thought, 'Oh, it won't matter if we let Lehman go. It's an investment bank.' But unfortunately when Lehman went, everyone decided, 'We're going to take our bat and ball home now.'

Hedge Fund Manager You had Lehman go down on Monday, AIG in trouble on Tuesday, the extent of HBOS's troubles were clear on Wednesday. Paulson had to go and see President Bush.

Author What did he say?

Hedge Fund Manager He used the phrase 'cardiac arrest'. 'Capitalism is having a cardiac arrest.' He needed Bush to understand, so he dramatised. He said, 'By the end of the week you won't be able to get cash from an ATM machine.

Young Man Funds were flowing out of Morgan Stanley, flowing out of Merrill, Goldman Sachs, Washington Mutual, billions a day.

Davies I'm on the board of Morgan Stanley and I can tell you we were on the phone . . .

Author Literally?

Davies Yes.

Author What happens?

Davies I'll tell you what happens. You pick up the phone, you call the US Treasury, you say, 'This is Morgan Stanley. We may be bust by the end of the week.' And the Fed were getting those calls from every bank in America.

Masa smiles.

Masa All we got was an email.

Author When, Masa?

Masa That day. That very day. We all got an email.

Author This was when you were working for Lehman Brothers?

Masa Yes. I'd been there for fourteen months.

Author So this was the 15th September?

Masa Yes. We went in that morning. There was silence. Then an email from New York saying, 'Thank you, you're on your own.'

Author And that was it?

Masa Next day the papers had photos of us leaving the building, with boxes which they said were full of our work.

Author I saw those photos. I remember them.

Masa Do you know what was in those boxes?

Author Tell me.

Masa What really happened: the canteen at Lehman worked on a credit system, so when we realised we had credit in the canteen, we all went down there. The boxes were full of Milky Ways and sandwiches and yoghurt. Because we were bankers, nobody called it looting.

Author What did you do that evening, Masa?

Masa I went to the Damien Hirst sale at Sotheby's. He sold a bull with two golden horns for 18.6 million dollars.

Author Goodness.

Masa If he'd had the sale a week later, he might have had to pay someone to take it away. Hirst was always a lucky artist.

The stage darkens.

Hedge Fund Manager And so that's when it happened.

Davies This is the situation. At this point nobody has any choice.

Young Man I'm not a conspiracy theorist. There are people who believe that Hank Paulson let Lehman go because Congress was reluctant to give him the money he needed, and he believed a small crisis would force Congress's hand. But this was a big crisis.

There is a long pause.

So.

Hedge Fund Manager At last, in comes the government. Putting money into all the banks. The Treasury's commit-ment to the free market had lasted precisely one day. On

Friday the world's only superpower was doing things it would have considered unthinkable on Monday. At the beginning of the week it could have dispatched its troubles by spending a few billion. By the end of the week it's spending seven hundred. And overnight, the US is a socialist country. It owns its banks. Having claimed all the advantages of the free market, all its benefits, not least for themselves, the bankers go running to the government saying, 'Give us some money. Gee whiz, you have to give us some money or we're going to go bankrupt. And when we go bankrupt we're going to drag everyone down with us.'

Author Blackmail.

Hedge Fund Manager Yes. Blackmail.

There's a moment's silence.

And observe, this is a new kind of socialism. Socialism for the rich. In Michigan, in Cleveland, they don't have socialism. They just have it on Wall Street. Everyone else is in as much trouble as ever.

And can I say, I believe this is the moment when a sense of injustice begins to kick in?

Music. Darker yet. Only Rudmann remains.

Rudmann I had a fantastic education. A fantastic education. I'm a red-blooded market-loving capitalist, make no mistake. But I also did PPE at Oxford, so I know there's more to life than what you learn at Harvard Business School. One of the things I learnt was that the purpose of government is to provide the public good. Things we all need: defence, education, health obviously. These things benefit us all, but it's not necessarily in anyone's direct commercial interest to provide them. And I would say, in the same way, the government's job is not just to regulate a financial system. It's also their job to provide it. Because a sound, reliable, decent financial system is what society needs if it's to function. In the last few years the banking system has been off God knows where, doing God knows what. And I suppose what offends me most is the sense of waste. I can see we have no choice but to prop up some of these bankers' mistakes. That's what we have to do. But what's difficult to swallow is that we're about to waste six trillion dollars doing it.

EIGHT

Music. The stage changes again. Davies returns to his blackboard.

Announcer Howard Davies, ex-diplomat, ex-Treasury, ex-Director General of the CBI, ex-Deputy Governor of the Bank of England, now Director of the London School of Economics.

Davies And so there it is. We reach Act Five.

Author Pumping.

Davies Yes. Pumping. Pumping money into the banks, and into the economy.

Author Quantitative easing?

Davies Helicopter money. The government's throwing money out of helicopters. And as in all Act Fives, there are bodies all over the stage.

Author Who are the bodies?

Davies RBS, HBOS, Lehman, Northern Rock, that's just to begin.

Author But surely if it's Act Five, isn't there a reckoning too?

Davies smiles.

Davies Well, that's a very good question. What a good question. Is there a reckoning?

A Financial Journalist comes on. She is gleaming, humorous, in her thirties.

Financial Journalist I think the story of Fred Goodwin tells you quite a lot.

Announcer Journalist. *Financial Times*. Firmly refuses to be identified.

Financial Journalist Do you know who he is?

Author Of course. Everybody knows Fred Goodwin.

Financial Journalist He was Chief Executive of RBS.

Author Sure. The one with the pension.

Financial Journalist That's him. And all the time I was working on his story, I kept remembering that remark of Andy Warhol's, perhaps you know it?

Author Andy Warhol said so many brilliant things.

Financial Journalist One of the things Warhol said was that people have sex in order to remind themselves of how good sex used to be.

Author That's very good.

Financial Journalist His way of putting it: 'Sex is nostalgia for sex.'

Author It's *very* good.

Financial Journalist In Fred Goodwin's case, it was the deal. Fred had risen to the top by making deals. So when the chance came along for RBS to buy a Dutch bank called ABN Amro, it was irresistible. And the fact that everyone was telling him he was mad, then that made the prospect even more delicious. That's how Fred had made his name in the first place. Bringing off impossible deals. He couldn't resist one more. The deal was nostalgia for the deal.

Cohen returns.

Announcer Ronald Cohen again.

Cohen Do you know Fred? I mean, personally?

Author I don't, no.

Cohen I suppose it's unlikely he'll agree to see you?

Author Do you know, I think it is. For a start, he's behind gates on the Riviera. I don't think I'd get past the Rottweilers.

Cohen If all of us exist between two axes – one axis is our interest in people, the other axis is our interest in results – then Fred's interest in results is one hundred and his interest in people is very low. I can't think of anything he's interested in more than results. He plotted the acquisition of ABN Amro with the excitement of a man who imagined the colony taking over the empire. A Scottish bank would become the largest in the world. And it was, technically, a very complicated bid, he had to lay off part with Santander, and sell another part to Fortis, and so the bid itself was a work of art, and most of all, getting it through was a great triumph over his rivals at Barclays. And that's all he saw. He didn't see that the deal was going to destroy his bank and drag it towards bankruptcy. That's where people get it wrong, when they talk about bankers being greedy. It's not greed.

Author It's power?

Cohen Not even that.

Author What then?

Cohen The thing itself. That's what it's about.

The Author turns back to the Financial Journalist.

Author Is it true Fred Goodwin was rehearsed?

Financial Journalist Oh, you've heard about that, have you?

Author I have.

Financial Journalist For his House of Commons appearance?

Author Yes.

Financial Journalist That's right.

Author What happened?

Financial Journalist Fred had to appear before a House of Commons Select Committee to explain why RBS had more or less destroyed the British economy. He had to be prepared for his appearance. He'd already hired a former editor of the *News of the World*, and so now he got a group of old RBS advisers to do a series of mock questionings with them acting the Committee. They had the best job in town: abusing Fred Goodwin for a living.

Author How did he take it?

Financial Journalist From what I've heard, he hated it. They told Fred Goodwin, you have to appear before the Committee and you have to say you're sorry. Fred said he wasn't sorry. They told him he had to say he was. Fred said he didn't want to. They said he had to. This went on for about an hour. Fred said, 'Why should I?' And then finally someone said, 'Because if you don't you will look like a total cunt.' And that's when Fred began to get it.

But beyond the 'sorry' issue, there was a more profound issue. Fred didn't think anyone had the right to ask him questions. Fred wasn't used to being questioned. They said to Fred, 'That's how democracy works. They have the right to ask these questions.' He replied, 'But that doesn't mean they should ignore the facts.'

Author What facts? I don't understand. These people bewilder me. They bewilder me.

Financial Journalist Why?

Author Am I going mad? This is a man who bought ABN Amro without noticing it was full of toxic debt. He destroyed his bank. He nearly destroyed the British economy. I've tried for three months, I've really tried, not to get angry. But what possible defence can Fred Goodwin have?

Financial Journalist For a start, he says it was a board decision. The Chairman signed off on it. And secondly, in the business conditions of the time, it was a good decision, and nobody could have foreseen the way things were going. I tell you, he's very, very angry.

Author *He's* angry?

Financial Journalist Sure.

Author What's he angry about?

Financial Journalist Principally Fred's angry at the markets for not behaving in what he regards as a rational manner. Plainly the disaster can't be his fault, because it's not possible he got anything wrong. So it must be someone else's. And that only really leaves the market. It can't be down to unforeseeable circumstances, because even if it *was* unforeseeable, he's Fred Goodwin and he would have foreseen it.

Author That's crazy. He can't be that crazy.

Financial Journalist Let me tell you, I talk to a lot of bankers, and I've yet to meet one who is in any way contrite. Not one who feels apologetic.

Author Why not?

Financial Journalist They just don't think they've done anything wrong.

Author They haven't done anything wrong?

Financial Journalist Oh look, they know they're not popular, that's why they're talking to journalists again. Suddenly my calls are returned. Because when financial people are on the way up, they don't need us. They think, 'I don't care what anyone thinks of me. If some poxy journalist wants to say I'm an arsehole, why should I care? I'm cleverer than they are. I must be cleverer than they are because I earn more money than they do, and anyway I'm in Monte Carlo with my vile friends.' I have to tell you I've been gobsmacked at the extent to which bankers don't get it. These people genuinely believe they're masters of the universe. And why are they masters of the universe? Because they're paid fifty times as much as anyone else. So they must be cleverer than anyone else.

Author Do they really think that?

Financial Journalist Why wouldn't they? No banker believes he's lucky. However much money they earn, they all believe they deserve it. This is the root of the thing. Their pay is not necessary. In a real market you say, 'How much do we need to pay the author to write this play?' You don't then say, 'Oh so let's pay him that times fifty.' From 2000 onwards the bank employment market ceased to be a genuine market. That's when bankers decided that because they were working in an ice cream factory, they could help themselves to as much ice cream as they liked. They came to believe that they made the money, not the company. And they're wrong. They make money *for* the company. But that's what they refuse to accept.

Author What do you mean, they don't accept it?

Financial Journalist They just don't accept it.

Author They have to accept it.

Financial Journalist Do they?

The Financial Journalist looks at the Author.

Tell me. Do *you* accept it?

Author Do *I* accept it?

Financial Journalist Sure. When you write a play and the critics say it's crap. Do you accept it?

Author Of course not. Of course I don't. I mean, absolutely not. Why would I? They're wrong. They're always wrong.

Financial Journalist Well, exactly. So how is this different?

Author Once you go down that path, accepting what critics say, grovelling to the audience, God, then you might as well shoot yourself. It's an end to self-respect.

Financial Journalist So? *So?* How are playwrights different from bankers? Isn't this about self-belief? A certain self-belief? Isn't that necessary? Isn't it necessary? To a banker? To a playwright?

Author Sure. Of course it is. But as far as I know playwrights don't make a living out of fucking up people's lives.

There is a long pause. The Author walks round but says nothing.

Financial Journalist All right, OK.

Author OK . . .

Financial Journalist I've hurt you.

Author No, honestly, you haven't hurt me.

Financial Journalist I tell you I used to drink with some friends from Oxford, and they'd all gone into the City, and I'd gone into journalism. And I used to say, 'My newspaper's parent company made God knows how many millions last year, but know what? I don't believe that money is morally mine. I believe it belongs to the company, not me.' And they would say, 'I'm going to have to quit where I work, no way I'm going to settle for half a million a year.' And I would say, 'Do you hear yourselves? *Do you hear yourselves?*'

The Author is pacing, disturbed.

Oh, and by the way, he later went back to them.

Author Sorry?

Financial Journalist Later on he went back to his advisers.

Author Who?

Financial Journalist Fred.

Author He went back?

Financial Journalist Apparently. That's the word.

Author What for?

Financial Journalist Because he was so pleased with how the House of Commons went. Of all the witnesses to the Committee, he was voted in a newspaper poll to be the most convincing. Fred went back to his advisers and said, 'Now I want you to help with my pension.'

Author And did they?

Financial Journalist They said, 'You want to hold on to your pension?' 'I do.' 'Two thousand pounds a day?' 'More or less.' 'You do know you could come in for quite a lot of stick?' 'That's fine. I want my pension more than I want to be popular.'

Tom Huish, from Birmingham, comes on.

Huish People who come to us fall into two groups. Either they have problems already – bereavement, unemployment, drugs, drink, family violence, mental illness. The latest misfortune – seeing their house repossessed, having their possessions taken away – is just one in a long line.

Announcer Tom Huish. Advisor. Citizens Advice Bureau, West Midlands.

Huish Or there's a second characteristic. They're in denial. The brown envelopes have been coming through the door for months. And they haven't opened them. They've ignored them, because in a very human way people believe that if they don't think about their problems, they'll go away. It's my job to advise people who to pay, and in what order.

Author What do I have to pay?

Huish Council tax. If you don't pay council tax, you go to jail. Also, remember, if it's just credit card debt, then the bailiffs are what you might call respectable bailiffs, they work for the magistrates' court, so they're salaried professionals. But the bailiffs who collect council tax, they've been privatised, so they're complete bastards.

Author So do I ever have to pay my credit card?

Huish It's up to you. The likelihood is, after a couple of months they'll sell your debt on.

Author They'll sell it on?

Huish Oh sure. If they can't collect it, they'll sell it to someone else. For fifty per cent, say. To another company. And when that happens you get visited by a new set of bailiffs. But then after a couple of months, they sell it on

64

again, this time for twenty per cent. And so on. And all the time the collector's paying less for the risk, so collecting the debt is becoming less urgent. So you could say in the long run the system works in your favour.

He smiles.

Sometimes you have to declare yourself bankrupt. But that's not so terrible. Nowadays even policemen are allowed to go bankrupt. In fact bankruptcy isn't a bar to any job any more. Except banking.

Simon Loftus appears, gym-fit and vigorous.

Loftus Fine. All I care about is pay. That's the only reason I wanted to be a trader. To be paid a lot of money.

Announcer Simon Loftus, bond trader, aged twenty-four.

Loftus If I'm not going to be paid a lot of money, I'll leave. I did three years of maths at Oxford. People say it's hard, but actually it's quite easy, unless you want to get a First. You can coast and get a 2:1. I went straight to a big American bank, trading government bonds. You don't have be a genius. It's an adrenaline business. When you've made money during the day, it's very satisfying. All you need is discipline. When you're trading you have to get out when you've planned to get out. Too many traders think, 'Oh why don't I hang on, maybe things'll get better.' No, you have to reach that point and out.

If you want to know what I think: I feel betrayed. Society over-borrowed, the banks were reckless, the politicians mismanaged the economy and at the end of it all my generation has missed the boat. We missed the good years. It was easy to be a trader when everything was going up. You couldn't get it wrong. Guys got amazing bonuses. I feel the baby-boomers have taken everything . . .

Author People like me.

Loftus Yes, absolutely. You've taken everything and you've left us with nothing. Only debt and more debt, with years to pay it off. I'm going to leave Britain. Let's face it, land of opportunity it ain't. What have we got? Enormous debt. High taxes. If I'm getting tagged fifty or sixty p, who wants that? Hong Kong is a no-brainer.

The Financial Journalist returns.

Financial Journalist There's a lot of deliberate helplessness, affected helplessness. Especially among politicians. The attitude is, 'What can you do? Nothing's going to work, how do you make laws against greed?' Bankers have done a brilliant job of making us all believe that this is a recession like any other. But it isn't. This recession was triggered by a breakdown in the financial system. If you legislate, you can do something to stop it happening again. But politicians don't have the will. Because, let's face it, politicians are thinking, 'When I leave office, hey, maybe I can sit on the board of a bank.'

NINE

Music. Masa and the Author only.

Masa And there it is, you see, that's the story.

Author Is that it?

Masa That's it.

Author What happens next?

Masa I can't tell you what happens next.

Author Why not?

Masa You haven't been listening. If the story has a moral it's that you come to grief when you try to predict the future.

They both smile.

Author Thank you very much. You've been fantastic.

Masa Thank you. Do you know what the story's about?

Author I would have thought so. I think I do. It's about the death of an idea, isn't it?

Masa Is it?

Author Yes.

Masa What idea?

Author Since the 1980s people have been saying that markets are decent and wise. And now we know they're not. They're not. No one can look you in the eye and say markets work. What is it Alan Greenspan says? 'The whole intellectual edifice has collapsed.'

Masa Did he say that?

Author It's in the research. Type it into Google – he said it. And that's what we've learnt. Markets are not decent and they're most certainly not wise. That idea is over. It's dead. It's lying dead on the stage.

Masa And?

Author And?

Masa What else? Tell me what else.

There's a silence. The Author thinks a moment. Then:

Author Oh . . .

One by one, in his memory, different people from the story appear.

Young Man One of the things I noticed was the people who didn't believe in the bubble – look at their names – Nouriel Roubini, Nassim Taleb – they come from societies which periodically collapse. Iran, Lebanon.

Freud I like working with Ronnie Cohen, because in a way we're the same. Ronnie and his family were kicked out of Egypt at the time of Suez. And my father was kicked out of Austria in 1938. We're refugees. It marks everything you do and everything you think. You see things more clearly.

Hammond They had to save the banking system. They had to. If they hadn't saved the system we would all have been sitting outside our houses guarding our food stocks with guns.

Lovelock After the Savings and Loan scandal, 3,630 bankers were put behind bars. Funny, haven't seen any handcuffs this time, have you?

Chair of a Mortgage Lender Everyone wants the bankers to say sorry. They're never going to say sorry. Because that's not what people do when they're attacked. If you attack someone they fight back. And the bankers feel under attack. Banking is a bold, adversarial world, it's not going to change when the going gets tough. If anything, the opposite.

Cohen I knew the crisis would come. It was just a question of when. But when I left my job, I didn't want to be the kind of man who predicts doom for everyone who follows him. So I said nothing.

Huish If a bailiff comes to your house, don't let them in. Sometimes they say they need to use the loo. Take it from me. They don't.

Loftus It's a generational thing, isn't it? You lot became artists. We became bankers.

Davies I like Alistair Darling. My friends in the Treasury tell me he wanders round the corridors saying, 'Well, I've been in the job two years and still nobody's told me where Gordon's hidden the money.'

Cruddas It's a shame we didn't have Blair, Cameron and Clegg all at the same time, then we would have had not just the same politics, but the same politician – same build, same suits, same hair.

Rudmann The UK economy is fucking toast, man. It's fucked. I'm off. I'll be gone in two years.

Freud I have no idea why we go round criticising the Chinese for not coming up to our standards on human rights. They're so soon going to be the dominant world power I think we should get used to the idea of being nice to them.

Masa My family escaped from Sarajevo after three years of war. I was ten. I went through a secret tunnel dug under the airport and over a mountain. Twelve thousand people died in a siege which lasted over four years. I don't know whether I should be happy I lived to tell the tale or resentful I have such a tale to tell.

Freud My proudest boast is, I got out of banking with my health, my wealth and my wife. Very few people can say that.

Turner I'm running the FSA and I come from the private sector myself but I do get tired of a certain private-sector arrogance. When people say, 'Oh get some private-sector people into the schools, that'll sort them out.' Actually I doubt if there are many jobs in finance as hard as teaching a class of fourteen-year-old boys in a tough school. Because business is in some ways quite simple, it has clearly defined aims. The aim is to make money. So you have a measure against which to judge all the subsidiary actions which add up to the overall result. Managing a hospital is rather more complex. Because it's very hard to know what your objective is. There's no money-metric to help make the choice between better cancer care or having a better A&E. It's a judgement call.

And running a hospital is an endless series of judgement calls where the criteria and objectives are very far from clear. So don't tell me that's easier than making money. Or that people whose responsibilities are hugely complicated can be 'sorted out' by people whose responsibilities have the benefit of being more clearly defined. And if at the end of all this the financial sector is smaller, and some clever people, rather than thinking of finance as the automatic profession of choice, decide to innovate pharmaceuticals or develop technologies to battle climate change, would that be a bad thing? Would it?

Financial Journalist The people I drink with, they say, 'It's so unfair. I'm only paid half a million.' And I say, 'Do you know what unfair is?' Perhaps that's why they don't drink with me any more.

Only the Author remains, with his notebook. A penthouse suite overlooking Central Park. A private dining room, superbly luxurious. A Secretary clicks her heels across the parquet.

Secretary Mr Soros will be with you in a moment.

The Author is left alone. Then George Soros appears, hand already outstretched.

Soros Ah, Mr Hare. Welcome.

Author How do you do?

Soros I got your letter. You're writing about the financial crisis. Please.

Soros gestures towards a long table. They sit at opposite ends.

In my view, people are now making bad decisions because they imagine the whole system can be put back together unchanged. But they're wrong. The moment is far too decisive for that. We will get weaker and China will get stronger. You saw the opening ceremony of the Olympics. It was intended to convey a message. It said, 'If you all make the right movement at the right time, and you all make those movements together, you will have a very successful show. But if you do anything different the show will not work.'

Author It's a scary message.

Soros Yes. Scary. A lot of Chinese watched and knew it was scary. Western capitalism thrived through individual achievement, Chinese capitalism will thrive through state achievement.

Author I've read you no longer invest in Russia.

Soros That's so.

Author Why not?

Soros I made the mistake of believing Russia was going over to real capitalism, not gangster capitalism. I thought the choice between two telecommunication companies was going to be a real capitalist choice. But the choice was fixed, and I got burnt. I lost a billion dollars.

Author Really?

A short pause.

What was it like? Losing a billion dollars?

Soros I don't like it. It annoys me greatly.

Author Could you sleep at night?

Soros Yes, I could sleep, but I was in a bad mood.

Author Did you raise your voice? Did you throw things?

Soros No. Maybe I would have got over it quicker if I had. Running a hedge fund is very bad for your ego. And when it gets good for your ego, that's when you fall flat on your face.

A Waiter has appeared, hovering.

Soros Do you need anything?

Author I need nothing at all.

The Waiter goes.

Soros You ask me if I know Alan Greenspan.

Author *Do* you know Greenspan?

Soros He and I have got closer. We had a one-to-one lunch in Zurich. He's in thrall to Ayn Rand – *Atlas Shrugged*, *The Fountainhead*, you know. He loves Rand's books, so he believes in creative destruction. When we met in Zurich it was before the present crisis, and at that lunch he said, 'Markets are imperfect but they bring such benefits that you just have to live with the fact that from time to time they collapse, so you just pick up the bits.' But then I saw him again recently – after the crisis. Shall I tell you what he said? He said 'What I said in June no longer applies.'

Author That's incredible.

Soros Yes, but even at the first lunch, the lunch in Zurich when he said, 'The benefits of the market are so great that you have to live with the price,' even then – even then I had an answer.

A silence.

Author What was your answer?

Soros My answer?

Author We want to know what you said.

Soros I said, 'Yes, but Alan, the people who end up paying the price are never the people who get the benefits.'

They start to eat.